1

Women and Foreign Policy

Women have a right to participation and leadership in American foreign policymaking as a matter of simple equity. Although women cannot be expected to speak with one voice or have identical beliefs or interests, we believe that if the time comes when we progress from tokenism to the presence of a 'critical mass' of women (as many as men) in government and public institutions, we will have foreign policies more rooted in the reality of people's needs, and our nation and the world will be a safer, healthier and better place in which to live.

—Women's Foreign Policy Council

IN THE UNITED STATES, and in most other countries, women have generally been excluded from the institutions that make and implement foreign policy and conduct war. This near ostracism from the centers of power and the agencies responsible for foreign affairs has meant that women have rarely been

This issue of the HEADLINE SERIES *was made possible by the generosity of the Board of Governors of the Off-The-Record Lecture Series.*

present when the most critical decisions a nation faces have been made, especially the decision to go to war. However, women have been, and still are, deeply affected by such foreign endeavors.

In the last two decades, a chorus of women's groups has become increasingly vocal in demanding a role for women in the critical decisions concerning war and peace. Some who argue for the inclusion of women in the foreign policy process take the position that women are innately or by socialization more peaceful than men, and that the different views of women need to be incorporated into decisionmaking. Others contend that as citizens women should be allowed to participate in the decisions affecting their lives and the future of their country and the world, regardless of whether their views differ from men's. While disagreeing about the reasons for including women, both camps do agree that by any measure women have been, and still are, woefully underrepresented in the conduct of foreign affairs.

This HEADLINE SERIES will explore several aspects of the situation of women in the U.S. foreign policy establishment. Why have women been excluded? How have the major institutions of foreign policy prevented women from assuming an equal role with men? What are the roads into the foreign policy establishment for women aspiring to play a role in international affairs? Where are the women who have made it into the foreign policy establishment currently to be found? What special attributes characterize these women on the inside of the policy process? And what is the future for women in foreign policy?

In search of answers, the authors have drawn on several sources, from current research studies to a series of interviews they conducted in 1988 and 1991 with women and men in positions of influence in the U.S. State and Defense departments. They consulted political appointees and career employees in the upper echelons of both departments (Senior Executive Service or SES and Senior Foreign Service or SFS), from assistant secretaries to ambassadors. Thus the interviewees were at the heart of the foreign policy process.

"Naturally you make less than the men, Miss Johnson—it's just not safe for a woman to carry around that much money these days."

The entire fabric of society in the United States has been organized around gender stereotypes, and these set the parameters within which individuals function by establishing differing patterns of behavior that are acceptable for men and women. Though gender stereotypes include a number of elements, this discussion will focus on three: the relationship of women to work; views on the suitability of women for work in foreign policy and its related fields; and society's expectations about men's and women's interests and capabilities.

'Women as Homemakers'

Historically, one of the most formidable barriers to women's entrance into the inner sanctum of foreign affairs has been the view that a woman's primary role was to be a mother and wife, and that work outside the home was to be avoided. Thus until recently only a minority of women chose to pursue full-time careers. Although in the 1990s few people still object to a married woman working, there continues to be a strongly held belief that it would be preferable for a woman to place her husband's wishes and her children's needs ahead of her career. For instance, in a 1989 Virginia Slims national poll, 62 percent of all women and 55 percent of all men responded that a wife should quit her job if her husband were transferred. On the other hand, only 29 percent of the women and 28 percent of the men in the same national sample felt a husband should quit his job and relocate if his wife were offered a very good job in another city. Relatedly, in a 1990 national survey reported in *Public Perspective*, 64 percent of the population felt it was better for the children if the mother stayed home and the father worked, and 41 percent thought it would be better if the man was the achiever outside the home and the woman took care of the home and family.

The stereotype that women should not work kept many from pursuing a career in the past. Even today some of the women interviewed in the State and Defense departments report that the expectation that women should subordinate their jobs to the needs of their spouse and children impacted on their careers. Several of them, for instance, indicated that they endured resistance to their working based on the stereotype that they should be at home:

> *It will almost sound silly, but when I first came back to work.... I was told 'The women who work here aren't, in large number, very good. What makes you think you'll be able to work the overtime?' At the time I had two small children and subsequent to that I was working very long hours, the same person, my boss, said to me, 'You must be a terrible wife and mother because you are here all the time.'*

Obviously this woman faced a difficult time not only in balancing her career and family obligations but also in confronting the negative views of her superior regarding her dual roles. (All interviewees were guaranteed anonymity because they feared that they could easily be identified, which could jeopardize their careers.) A political appointee in the Defense Department experienced the conflict more directly, admitting that she delayed the high-powered stage of her career while her children were young:

I would not have done this [taken the appointment] if they [her children] had been younger. My husband was the greatest supporter.... If they [the children] were young he would have probably said, 'You go, I'll raise them.' But there is a certain point when you wouldn't have done that, when they were little. I just couldn't do it.

'Unsuited to Diplomacy'

While certain stereotypes about the place of work in women's lives are fast fading, a more persistent and damaging set of views concerns the belief that women are incapable of doing the work required of career diplomats. It has been assumed in many countries that only men could serve as diplomats for the king or government, and diplomacy has been portrayed as the job of men in high hats and striped pants. This cultural view seems related to the notion that only men can confront the enemy in military battle. The tie between the two can be found in the historical linkage of the roles of soldier and citizen. More specifically, the right to participate in the making of a country's foreign policy has been predicated on the ability to fight in a country's wars.

The founders of the United States believed in the tie between citizenship and fighting to defend the country and drew heavily on this philosophical tradition in drafting their new constitution. Most accepted the idea that politics, war and, by extension, foreign policy were properly the arena for men. Americans in the twentieth century have not completely rid themselves of this view. The 1989 Virginia Slims survey previously mentioned asked a national sample if women in public office could do a better, worse or just as good a job as men in several select areas. Fifty-eight percent of men and 42 percent of women thought a woman would do a worse job than a man in directing the military; 23 percent of men and 17 percent of women thought a woman would not be as good as a man in conducting diplomatic relations with other nations; and 37 percent of men and 24 percent of women believed a woman would be worse in making decisions about going to war. Thus, many in the public see women as ill-equipped to exercise power in foreign or military conflicts, which is the very essence of international relations.

Further support for the existence of these stereotypes can be seen in the recent controversy about allowing women, or forcing women, to serve in military combat or to be drafted. In the aftermath of the invasion of Panama in 1989 and Operation Desert Storm in 1991 there has been considerable discussion about the combat ability of women. Reporters (including, incidentally, a growing number of women) who covered both conflicts wrote of the key roles played by women. After the Persian Gulf war was over, the issue of combat exclusion was taken up by some members of Congress, notably Representative Patricia Schroeder (D-Col.), who introduced legislation to open up to women some formerly closed job titles, potentially involving women in combat. The resulting opposition from the public, politicians and military leaders was testimony to the deep-seated beliefs about women, men and war. While a *Newsweek Magazine* poll in 1991 found only 44 percent of the public rejected the idea of the assignment of women to ground combat units, a majority believed only women who wanted such assignments should be given them. Moreover, 89 percent expressed concern about women leaving small children at home, 53 percent doubted women would be able to perform at the same level as men, and 51 percent thought allowing women to serve as infantry soldiers would be a burden on the military. Thus, although Congress passed legislation in 1991 that repealed the ban on women flying combat planes in the Navy and Air Force, it did not mandate such a policy. Rather, it established a commission to further investigate the issue. The commission, appointed by President George Bush (1989–93) and weighted with conservatives, recommended not allowing women to fly in combat or fight on the ground, although it did say women should be allowed to serve on some military ships. While split, a majority of the commission argued that allowing women to serve in combat would have a negative impact on military readiness, cohesiveness and effectiveness. In 1993, the late Secretary of Defense Les Aspin finally removed the ban on women flying combat planes and was instrumental in getting legislation passed that allowed women to serve on combat ships. While many in Congress and the public still see this as a dangerous change of policy, Secretary Aspin argued, "We know from experience that women can fly our high-performance fighter aircraft. We know from experience that they can perform well in assignments at sea. And we know from Operation Desert Storm...that women can stand up to the most demanding environments. So we're acting on what we know."

'Women Know Less'

Society's perception of foreign policy as a career unsuited to women is not conditioned solely by attitudes about women's military abilities. Another problem is the general belief that women are less knowledgeable than men about foreign affairs. Public opinion polls have generally found much higher levels of information and opinion on foreign affairs among men than women, and as a result, both the public and policymakers tend to assume that all women are less knowledgeable than men. This attitude was perhaps most succinctly revealed in comments by Donald T. Regan, chief of staff for President Ronald Reagan (1981–89). At the first summit meeting between Reagan and Soviet President Mikhail S. Gorbachev in Geneva, Switzerland, Regan told reporters that women would rather read the "human-interest stuff" about Nancy and Raisa and would not "understand throw-weights or what is happening in Afghanistan or what is happening in human rights." Assemblywoman Maxine Waters (D-Cal.) was quick to note that opinions like Regan's are clearly detrimental to women wishing to influence diplomatic policy. "To indicate that women don't have the intellectual capability to understand what's happening here is certainly an insult. It means someone is trying to make us believe we don't know enough to be involved, and it would be a sad state of affairs if people really believe the myth." This stereotype surfaced during Geraldine Ferraro's vice presidential debate with Bush when she was asked whether she would "know what to do to protect this nation's security" or whether the Soviets "might be tempted to try to take advantage of you simply because you are a woman?"

Unfortunately, much of the general public and public officials do believe "this myth." This view is augmented by the cultural stereotype that women lack an aggressive demeanor and the ability to negotiate with, or stand up to, an enemy. Thus, women seeking careers in foreign policy continue to find themselves hampered by persistent stereotypes about the appropriateness of their choice.

The stereotype of foreign policy as a male preserve, coupled with the notion that women are not knowledgeable about foreign affairs, is the preconception that created the most difficulty for the women in the authors' foreign policy research. Several respondents drew the connection between these views and their own problems in establishing credibility within the foreign policy establishment. A respondent in the Defense Department noted that as a result of these stereotypes "there is a natural tendency of people on meeting a woman in the Defense Department to assume that she is a secretary, or of low level, until there is evidence to the contrary." Elaborating on this idea, a woman whose expertise is in nuclear weapons commented, "It doesn't matter internally because I'm a known quantity. But when I go out of house and have to deal with new admirals, I have to establish my credibility to convince them." When asked if her area of expertise made this a particular problem, she answered, "Yes, because it is very technical; it is very masculine, it is very macho. What can be more macho than nuclear warheads exploding?" Even a woman as close to the inner circle of foreign policy as Jeane Kirkpatrick was during the Reagan Administration (she served as the U.S. Representative to the United Nations and a member of the National Security Council) often felt the pressure of these stereotypes. She reported:

> *You get the feeling that you are under continuous scrutiny of a critical nature.... I believed there was a little more resistance to accepting women as experts. I noticed this a lot about [British Prime Minister] Margaret Thatcher, a lot of a tendency to suggest that if a woman is strong, she's seen as tough. If she's strong enough to be in the job, then she's tough, which is never a compliment. But if she's not strong, she's not strong enough to be in the job. If you are assertive enough to demonstrate expertise, you are likely to be charged with lecturing or being schoolmarmish. But if you are not, then you're likely to be regarded as not a factor, not sufficiently either expert or strong enough to be a factor. I think that there are a number of this kind of 'double binds' for women in public life.*

As implied by Kirkpatrick, another societal value limiting women's roles in foreign policy concerns expectations about women's interpersonal skills, or capabilities as managers. Women are seen as more nurturant and men as better leaders and managers. Strongly held negative stereotypes about women managers create a particular problem for women who seek positions in the upper echelons of the government. A 1989 poll asked people to indicate whether they associated certain traits with a female or male boss or manager. Among those seeing a difference between men and women bosses (over 40 percent of the sample), men thought men managers would be better than women managers in terms of 10 of 14 attributes. Even women gave men the advantage on seven of the items. Men were generally seen as tougher, better informed, more decisive, better in dealing with competitors and more respected by those who report to them. Women bosses were given the advantage in the areas of honesty, concern with workers' rights and employees' personal problems. These stereotypes indicate that society perceives women as better equipped to handle the "soft" issues in politics and management (employees' personal issues) than the "hard" issues involving conflict (dealing with competitors or managing the military).

For the women who do advance into managerial positions, the weight of these stereotypes can be very burdensome. The senior women executives at State and Defense indicated they sometimes felt the limitations imposed by these views. As one explained:

> *Every woman is always aware of the stereotype that she is going to be more emotional, perhaps less steady, and softer on the issues. I think a lot of women in positions of importance have to be aware that that is there. Perhaps they compensate, perhaps they don't.*

In conclusion, these cultural stereotypes culminate in widespread discrimination against women seeking jobs in government and, more particularly, foreign affairs. The 1989 Virginia Slims survey, for instance, found that when presented with a list of 11 areas where women faced discrimination, more than half the women claimed that women faced problems in obtaining top jobs in government and in the military services. Ninety percent of the women in the same poll believed that major or at least some changes were needed with respect to opportunities for women in leadership positions in government in the next 10 years. A survey of women already working in the government by the U.S. Merit Systems Protection Board in 1990 substantiated this perception. Only a third felt that women and men are equally respected. As President Bill Clinton's former press secretary Dee Dee Meyers, the first woman and the youngest person to serve in that job, noted: "Women, and particularly young women, have a little bit more trouble being taken seriously, being afforded the authority that you need to do this job."

Thus even though many people would like to see a foreign policy arena in which women and men are equal players, cultural norms have served in the past to limit women's access to the circle of foreign policymakers and to inhibit the influence of those few women who make it into the inner sanctum. However, cultural views are only part of the answer to why so few women have played a role in setting U.S. foreign policy. Just as critical in explaining the absence of women have been the organizational practices of the foreign policy establishment that have discriminated, often legally, against women.

2

Gender and the Foreign Policy Institutions

RELATIONS AMONG COUNTRIES have frequently been called "high politics," since foreign policy choices can be some of the most momentous decisions a national government can make. The consequences, in terms of the benefits of peace or the costs of conflict, can be enormous. As a result, foreign policy decisions are usually taken at the highest level of government. However, in the American system, power to make foreign policy has never been specifically located.

Under the Constitution, the responsibility for foreign policy formulation has been divided between the President and the Congress. Over time, the dominance of the President in this process grew, while the influence of Congress declined. In part, this was due to congressional willingness to abrogate responsibility for difficult decisions. Correspondingly, this also reflected the increased importance of the United States as a major actor in world politics and the resultant necessity for quick decisions

"Not so fast...she pays well, benefits are generous and there's no glass ceiling."

and rapid actions for which the office of the presidency was best suited. This process peaked in the "Imperial Presidency" of the Johnson-Nixon era of 1963–74. More recently Congress has used a variety of its powers to reassert its role in foreign policy. Indeed the current Republican majority in the Congress has proposed legislation that would in a major way strengthen the congressional role. A House bill would cut funding for many foreign programs and eliminate several agencies in the foreign policy establishment. Secretary of State Warren Christopher is quoted by Congressional Quarterly as saying the bill "wages an extraordinary assault on this and every future President's constitutional authority to manage foreign policy."

The shifting balance of power between the executive and congressional branches has also been mirrored in the changing power of the relevant governmental institutions. Throughout U.S. history, the institution which has almost exclusively controlled the foreign policy process has been the State Department. Organized around the Foreign Service and the nation's ambassadors, the State Department has been uniquely suited to formulate and implement foreign policy. However, recent developments have led to a decline in the department's influence and a corresponding rise in the power of the White House and the Pentagon. Much of this trend has been attributed to the personalities of recent Presidents, such as Richard M. Nixon, Jimmy Carter, Ronald Reagan and George Bush. This shift can also be seen as a result of the function of the State Department itself, with its relatively passive role of observation, reporting and negotiation, as compared with the Defense Department's primary function of action. Particularly during internationally activist Administrations, the military has become the largest implementer of foreign policy decisions. Additionally, recent reorganizational measures, which have consolidated five of the nine intelligence agencies within the Department of Defense, have made the Pentagon into the largest gatherer and supplier of information for the formulation of foreign policy. Thus, today both executive-branch departments, State and Defense, are major foreign policy agents.

In addition to these two departments, recent Presidents have increasingly relied on the staff of the National Security Council (NSC) to aid in the formulation and occasionally implementation of foreign policy. The NSC is a relatively recent innovation, having been created in 1947 as an institution that would allow Presidents to avoid the bureaucratic quagmire often found in Foggy Bottom (a sobriquet for the State Department) and the Pentagon. Composed of the President and the Vice President, the secretaries of State and Defense, and assisted by the chairman of the Joint Chiefs of Staff and the director of the Central Intelligence Agency, the NSC has become an important player in making foreign policy under recent Presidents.

The Congress also has a constitutional role to play in determining the foreign policy of the nation. It alone can declare war. Additionally, all treaties and presidential appointments to executive agencies and, more specifically, ambassadorships must receive Senate approval. In recent years, Congress has voted to withhold monies to force a change in some Presidents' foreign policies. Several congressional committees, as a result, have become prominent actors. The continuing influence of Congress is reflected not only in the traditionally powerful Senate Foreign Relations and House Armed Services (now National Security) committees but also in the intelligence committees and appropriations committees in both the Senate and House. Lawmakers have, on occasion, relied on their power of the purse to do battle with the President over the direction of foreign policy.

Past and Current Practices

The federal government has long recognized that women in its employ are treated unequally. A 1992 study by the U.S. Merit Systems Protection Board found that women are prevented from moving to the upper echelons of government service in large part due to the attitudes and stereotypes of supervisors who believe women are less committed to the workplace than men. The same study reports that women in the government are aware of this "glass ceiling": more than half agree with the statement that "a woman must perform better than a man to be promoted."

All four institutions, the departments of State and Defense, the NSC and the relevant committees in Congress that form the core of the foreign policy structure, have a historical record of discrimination, direct or indirect, against women. The State and Defense departments went so far as to adopt specific policies to prohibit women from entering or to restrict the influence and opportunities of those women who were already employed. The State Department has been the target of lawsuits seeking to eliminate its discriminatory practices in hiring, promotions and assignments of women. As a result of court orders, the State Department has been revising the Foreign Service exam, as well as its appointment, review and promotion processes. Similarly, the Defense Department and its military branches virtually excluded women until very recently and are still wrestling with the implications of the policies that prohibit women from many combat positions. While the NSC and Congress did not adopt specific policies prohibiting women from serving, indirect discrimination has meant that few women until recently have made it into the inner circle of either organization. In the NSC, at least, this is changing. In the Clinton Administration, a number of women have been appointed to key positions, including the No. 3 staff job.

A related problem for women employed by the federal government is sexual harassment. Societal stereotypes have created a climate in which women have become the targets of unacceptable behavior. A 1980 study by the U.S. Merit Systems Protection Board of over 20,000 federal employees discovered that 42 percent of female employees and 15 percent of male employees reported having been sexually harassed in the previous 24 months. Similarly, a 1989 survey by *Government Executive Magazine* of 941 of the highest-ranking women government executives reported that 40 percent felt they had been sexually harassed.

Past Practices at State

Homer Calkin in his book on women in the State Department concluded that the field of foreign policy, and in particular the State Department, had been especially inhospitable to women. Calkin reported that it was 1922 before the department appointed Lucile Atcherson as its first woman Foreign Service Officer (FSO). The reason for the delay was, in part, tied to the late acceptance of women as full-fledged voting citizens, with all the rights of men to participate in politics (the Nineteenth Amendment had only become the law of the land in 1920). Even with enactment of the Nineteenth Amendment, however, the State Department was reluctant to hire women as FSOs because it felt they lacked the ability to do the job. The reasons given parallel the cultural stereotypes reviewed in the preceding chapter: once women married they would leave their posts; women could not handle the unfavorable climatic conditions in various parts of the world; and cultural prejudices in other nations against women would make them unsuitable government representatives. In light of these rationales, the State

Department Personnel Board even suggested applying for an executive order specifically excluding women from the department. As an alternative, it was proposed by Wilbur J. Carr, director of the Consular Service, that the department could use the entrance examination as a means of keeping women out. While no such explicit policy was adopted, the results suggest just such a practice was followed. Between 1926 and 1929, only four women were appointed to the Foreign Service, and from 1930 to 1941, no women were admitted.

A major policy shift took place in 1946 with the passage of the Foreign Service Act, which established the goal of a Foreign Service broadly representative of the American people. As a result, during the 1950s and 1960s more women were admitted to the State Department. However, the department continued to discriminate against women. Indeed, from 1960 to 1970, the percentage of women Foreign Service Officers actually declined from 9.2 percent to 4.8 percent. In reaction to this lack of progress, in 1970 the Ad Hoc Committee to Improve the Status of Women in Foreign Affairs Agencies was created, with the goal of ending discrimination in the State Department, the U.S. Agency for International Development (AID) and the U.S. Information Agency (USIA). This committee later became known as the Women's Action Organization (WAO). The WAO was instrumental in urging the department to take steps to encourage the recruitment of qualified women and to provide more training for women. As an early organizer, Mary S. Olmsted explained:

I think that in the beginning the WAO made people focus on what was really an appalling array of discriminatory attitudes and policies against women. A lot of people who were not in any way feminists had to admit that women were getting a very raw deal.... Assignments to positions illustrate the point...

It used to be that women were not assigned to certain posts, Moscow for instance. It was very, very rare to have a woman on a selection board up until the time WAO started protesting about that issue. It was hard for a woman to get university training. We broke down the ban against women Foreign Service Officers being married. Another problem WAO tackled was cone assignments, or assignments to functional specialties.... Traditionally, women officers were concentrated in the consular and administrative cones, although a limited number, myself included, spent their careers in the economic or political cones.... WAO also worked to improve the status of secretaries. Further, WAO pressed for better housing overseas and improved shipping allowances for single people (mostly women).

Throughout the 1970s, the State Department professed a willingness to help women, with Secretary of State Cyrus Vance in particular urging the department to make a special effort to hire qualified women. Vance created a committee, the Executive Level Task Force on Affirmative Action, with Ambassador Philip C. Habib as chairman, to review the recruitment and examination procedures in the State Department. The committee made recommendations designed to ensure that the service become "truly representative of American diversity." Yet in its report on conditions in the department, the Commission on Civil Rights found that "what some identify as traditional elitist attitudes have combined to limit severely employment opportunities for women and minorities in the Foreign Service."

Dissatisfied with State's progress toward the goal of diversity, Congress passed the Foreign Service Act of 1980, which required the Department of State to take steps to increase equal opportunities for women and minorities. Mary Olmsted and her colleagues reported that this legislation represented the first time Congress had required affirmative-action steps of a specific federal department. As a result of this legislation, there has been some movement toward increasing the number of women at State. However, Olmsted et al. concluded in their review that "the progress in the improvement in the status of women in the [State] Department continues to be agonizingly slow. If this rate should continue, it will be decades into the twenty-first century before women can expect to be represented equitably and to play a significant role in foreign affairs." Two 1989 studies (one by a five-member commission authorized by Congress, the other an internal State Department study) both concluded that the department was still failing to recruit sufficient women and minorities. While the Clinton Administration has made efforts to rectify this by appointing more women to the State Department, the President has placed many fewer women in high positions in State than he has in several other departments.

Current Practices at State

Not surprisingly, given the historical treatment of women in the department, State has been the target of legal challenges. Two early lawsuits were particularly important in this litigation effort to reform the department. In August 1971, the first major sex discrimination case filed against the State Department was decided in favor of Foreign Service Officer Alison Palmer. An expert on African affairs, Palmer was the subject of repeated acts of sexism from her initial appointment to the Foreign Service in 1958. However, unlike many of her contemporaries, she did not lightly dismiss the behavior of her male superiors. She claimed that she was denied appointment as a political officer by the U.S. ambassadors in Ethiopia, Tanzania and Uganda because she was a woman. One ambassador told her "the savages in Ethiopia would not be receptive to a woman, except maybe to her form." In compensation, Palmer was awarded a promotion, back pay and a desired assignment to the National War College. State conceded that there had been discrimination, but promised that changes would be made so that diplomats could no longer request that women be excluded from certain assignments. However, in 1976 Palmer was compelled to file her second lawsuit, a class action suit joined by the WAO. This suit was combined with another class action, *Cooper* v. *Baker*, and *in toto* they alleged that the State Department discriminated in hiring, assignments, performance ratings and awards. The State Department was found to have violated Title VII of the Civil Rights Act of 1964 and to have engaged in gender discrimination in a wide range of activities, including the Foreign Service exam, assignments, evaluations and awards. As a result of this case, two independent experts were to examine department processes and suggest modifications in its personnel system. The department canceled the 1989 Foreign Service exam since it had been found to be unfair to women and minority candidates. In May 1990 the U.S. Court of Appeals concluded that women were hampered in promotions due to fewer honor awards, service in less prestigious assignments and discriminatory evaluations. As a result of the ruling in *Palmer* v. *Baker*, 26 superior honor awards were conferred upon women who had been initially passed over. The State Department also notified 601 women that they might be entitled to compensation. As of May 1994, compensatory relief measures had been provided to over 200 women. In a subsequent case, the Voice of America and its parent organization, USIA, were likewise found to have been guilty of sex discrimination and ordered to compensate the victims.

In many ways Palmer deserves the major credit for forcing State to face up to its discriminatory treatment of women. It has not been easy for her, and the rewards have been few. Indeed, she left the Foreign Service feeling that her prospects had been irretrievably damaged. Throughout it all, she has had little support from the other women in State, a phenomenon she is at a loss to understand. But as she explains: "If I hadn't fought it, widespread discrimination would have continued forever. I would have been ashamed."

Unfortunately discriminatory practices seem to have continued. The department has been the target of an increasing number of Equal Employment Opportunity (EEO) complaints in the last decade: 25 in 1983; 32 in 1987; 55 in 1988; and in 1989, 75 informal leading to 42 formal. The pace has not abated: from 1989 to 1993, there was a 40 percent increase in the number of formal complaints. The most frequently cited issues in dispute were reprisal actions, conditions of employment, promotions and performance levels.

Similarly, nearly one third of the women interviewees at

State felt they had been discriminated against while working there. Several interviewees cited the former rule that all women had to resign from the Foreign Service when they got married. That practice stopped in the 1970s and some returned to work. Many more women undoubtedly left State permanently because of the marriage rule. Perhaps still others postponed or never married because of the ban.

Women with long careers in the State Department also recalled that when they were first in the Foreign Service, efforts were made to limit their rotation or early training to the traditional women's fields of consular affairs and administration. Typical is the response of a woman in her seventies when questioned as to whether she had ever faced discrimination (although often the older women did not recognize these practices at the time as sex discrimination):

> *I found as I was coming up in the ranks that I usually had to accept a position at a grade lower than my personal grade, whereas men usually did not have to. When I went out to India as a Class 3 officer, I had to take a Class 4 officer's job, but while I was there, I worked myself up into a Class 2 officer's job. I once asked for an assignment as economic counselor in Beirut. This was back when Beirut was still a lovely city, and assignments there were sought after. The person who was handling Lebanese affairs in the geographic bureau at the time said that over his dead body would the department send a woman to Beirut. Hence I did not get the assignment. My name was put forward as ambassador to Bangladesh, and there was considerable objection to that, although a woman got the job several years later. I am sure that I was the first woman ever proposed for that position and I was turned down cold....*

The stereotype that other cultures will not accept women Foreign Service Officers has been a problem for many females in the State Department. Because success in overseas assignments in key missions is so important for progressing up through the ranks, the inhospitable (or perceived inhospitable) environment in other nations for women in positions of authority can be and has been a problem.

In the same vein, sexual harassment has also been an issue for women at State. The department issued its first policy statement prohibiting sexual harassment and establishing procedures for the filing of formal complaints in 1981. Despite such policies, sexual harassment remains widespread. Indeed, as reported in *USA Today*, 52 percent of women employees claimed to have experienced sexual harassment while working in the State Department, the largest proportion of women employees in any government agency.

In general, however, women at State interviewed by the authors were positive about their status. When asked to evaluate the level of discrimination in their department on a seven-point scale (with one as severe discrimination and seven as equal treatment), the women at State gave an average score of 5.0. This was only slightly lower than their ranking for the government as a whole and better than the ranking they gave the country. A few, however, were quick to point out that the department was not exactly a leading government agency in improving women's status. "Only when forced does State do better.... Except when a Court tells them to do something, they wouldn't do it on their own." However, the women at State were in general agreement with the proposition that things for women were improving. However, the intractable nature of the problems for women can be seen in the fact that in 1993 a group of female Foreign Service Officers accused the department and Secretary of State Christopher of violating the previous antidiscrimination ruling, and they sought a five-year extension of the court's injunction prohibiting discrimination.

As of 1995 the Clinton Administration has decided to enter into global-settlement negotiations in an attempt to resolve all of the discrimination issues of *Palmer* v. *Baker* (now *Palmer* v. *Christopher*) in one consent decree. The settlement would include both specific relief for women officers as well as overall changes in the department's evaluation process in an attempt to make it more objective. The department has created a new diversity training program for all officers. However, as one of the lawyers involved in the litigation noted, the women in the department are facing an increased backlash from male colleagues, and a number of women have refused to accept court-ordered promotions due to the perception among fellow officers that they might not have deserved them.

Past Practices at Defense

As Maj. Gen. Jeanne Holm, USAF (Ret.), described in her comprehensive history of women in the military, the barriers placed in the way of women who wanted to enter the military side of the foreign policy establishment have been even steeper than those faced by women at the State Department. She concluded: "The story of women's progress is a marvelous tale of persistence, courage and foresight in the face of repeated frustrations and the built-in institutional resistance of the tradition-bound military subculture."

Women first began to play a recognized role in the nation's military during the Civil and Spanish-American wars as nurses. But nurses had no regular organizational structure until 1901, when Congress established the Nurse Corps as an auxiliary of the U.S. Army. The nurses, however, had no military rank, nor did they receive any of the military benefits.

The War Department initially resisted employing civilian women in any positions other than nurses. Only after suffering severe personnel shortages during World War I were the commanders able to convince the War Department to employ civilian women in clerical positions and other support roles. However, the War Department still rejected the concept of women serving permanently in the military, and it deactivated the women at the end of World War I. In fact, in 1925 the Naval Reserve Act of 1916 was even altered to require the employment of male citizens, so that the Navy could not even enlist Yeomanettes again.

Needless to say, this rejection of women, despite their contributions, was not popular with many women's groups. In an attempt to pacify them, the War Department in 1920 established a Director of Women's Programs, U.S. Army, with the limited purpose of serving as a liaison between the War Department and women's organizations. Instead, the director used the position to demand that the Army give greater recognition to women and began organizing the Women's Service Corps as an agency with full military status.

Even though World War II saw a large expansion of roles for women, the War Department was still unwilling to include women in the regular services. The compromise proposal was for the creation of an auxiliary of highly educated women. Thus, in the early 1940s, the Women's Army Corps (WAC), the Navy women's reserve (WAVES), the Coast Guard women's reserve (SPARS), the Marine Corps women's reserve and the Air Force civilian Women's Air Service Pilots (WASPS) were established. Yet women faced continued hostility for invading male preserves. Commented General Holm:

> *Reception by the men ranged from enthusiasm through amused condescension to open hostility. Each found that she had to prove herself each time she went to a new job or had a change in supervisors. Whereas a man was accepted immediately at face value and was assumed to be competent at his job, a woman was always regarded with suspicion. Because it was considered unnatural for a woman to join the military, she was often considered a deviate of some sort.*

Even though the standards for women officers and enlisted women were higher than those for men, military men in general believed that most jobs in their professions were inherently masculine, and they would not accept the possibility that they could be performed by women. Holm reported, "Like the male Marine Corps office clerks in World War I who estimated it would take two women to replace one male marine at a desk, most men genuinely believed the masculine mythology of the military world."

The War Department's treatment of black women was even worse. Most commanders refused to accept African-American women in their units, and those who did often employed them in stereotypical positions. For example, 60 black medical technicians in the WAC were put to work cleaning, rather than in practicing their medical specialties. When they began a sit-down strike, they were told that "'black girls' are 'fit only to do the dirtiest type of work' because that's what 'Negro women are used to doing.'"

By the end of World War II, acceptance of women was still limited. Even the wartime directors of the WACs, WAVES, SPARS and women marines did not ask for the retention of the women's units. However, in 1948, perhaps in response to the cold war, Congress passed the Women's Armed Services Integration Act, opening up the military services to women, but only in a very limited way. Women were to remain segregated in their own divisions, they were not to constitute more than 2 percent of the military, and women officers could not be promoted beyond the rank of lieutenant colonel/commander, except for the colonel/captain director of each women's branch. Not until the Vietnam War was there any major change in women's role in the military. In November 1967, President Lyndon B. Johnson signed Public Law 90-130, which removed restrictions on the careers of female officers in the Army, Navy, Air Force and Marine Corps by repealing the limits on the percentage of women in the services and barriers to their promotion. The traditional "slotting" of women into certain positions was also eased, although the resistance of male military officers and enlisted men persisted.

Throughout the 1970s women's progress in the military was relatively rapid as many of the old barriers were eliminated as a result of court decisions, the threat of legal action or executive initiatives. The adoption in 1973 of the All Volunteer Force also expedited the progress of women. The results of these changes were dramatic. By 1985 women's share of all active-duty military positions had increased to almost 10 percent.

The election of President Reagan brought a temporary halt to women's advancement, partially as a result of a review of women in the military conducted at Defense Secretary Caspar

W. Weinberger's request. The study reflected the earlier philosophy that it was preferable to have men rather than women in the services. However it soon became clear that the Administration could not achieve its policy of expanding the military without women. The Defense Advisory Committee on Women in the Services continued to push for changes to improve the status and opportunities of women, and in January 1988 the Task Force on Women in the Military recommended policies that would reduce sexual harassment and increase career opportunities. As noted earlier, the Clinton Administration took one step toward the latter by eliminating the ban on women serving as combat pilots and on combat ships. This is an important change because from the perspective of women in the military the combat exclusion has had a very detrimental influence. As Retired Brig. Gen. Evelyn P. Foote noted:

As long as women are operationally excluded, they will never acquire the experience that leads to their acquiring rank of more than one star. Unless they get the operational experience, they will never be in a position to have a significant impact on national defense policy....

The women absolutely hate combat exclusion, because it is an artificial barrier.... The women who serve the combat forces forward are not given credit for being in combat. They are in combat, and if they are attacked, they will attack back.

Civilian women at Defense frequently cite the organizational bias against women and their consequent lack of military, especially combat, experience as reasons for the difficulties they face working for the department. A woman in the naval-weapons area outlined the problem:

The military themselves have discrimination against civilians, whether they're male or female, because most civilians have not been in operations. So there is that bias or perception that civilians don't know what they're talking about. Then when you put the women on top of that, it makes it even a little worse. Department of Defense is a very macho world.... If the military stays male, women will always be less effective because they have not had to demonstrate to peers, to male peers, that they know what they are talking about because they have not been 'under fire.' Put it in quotes because there's a lot of men who have not been under fire either.

Current Practices at Defense

The Defense Department has faced a significant number of EEO complaints but only a few lawsuits. However, the level of discrimination in the Navy was revealed in November 1991 with the resolution of an 18-year-old lawsuit for sex discrimination in hiring and promotions. In finding for the plaintiffs, Judge Harold Green complained that "the government has sought to prolong this litigation by every means possible, both fair and foul."

Discrimination has also been a problem for civilian employees. More than half of the women interviewed at Defense (69 percent of those in career positions) stated that they had experienced sex discrimination. They complained about slow promotions or a failure to be moved up in rank. Others discussed experiences where their orders were challenged or senior colleagues refused to deal with a woman. The slow effort to build credibility, moreover, was frequently negated when women had to deal with men outside of their circle of associates. One woman's experience is typical. "If they know your expertise, they will listen to you. They will ask your advice. Often if you walk into a room of strangers, however, they merely will just assume you are a secretary."

In a study reported in *The Washington Post* in 1989, of 941 of the highest ranking women in the military, nearly 70 percent said their views were not as respected as men's. The problem is further exacerbated for the women civilian policymakers who do not have military credentials. Indeed, the failure to let women serve in equal numbers and positions with men in the military presents a double burden for women civilians. The women who discussed this problem indicated that as a result of their lack of "surface" credibility, they had a hard time proving themselves to their colleagues.

Perceived or anticipated sexual discrimination by male foreign nationals, a problem at State, was also identified by the women at Defense as a problem. For instance, a woman told the following story:

> *When I first started in this area, some stupid man got a hold of my boss and said, 'Oh the Japanese won't deal with a woman.' I had already been there several times and the ambassador and his deputy had asked me to come back because I was negotiating something for the Japanese they hadn't been able to get done. I had to overcome that silly stuff.*

Older men or those whose backgrounds did not involve working with women were a source of complaints for some women. As one woman described the situation:

> *A lot of our political appointees now, because of the restrictions on going to work for companies afterward and ethics, and the 'revolving door,' tend to be retired people. Now retired people in their sixties, let's say, have not worked with many women in industry in responsible positions. They're not very much used to it. They tend not to take you seriously.*

Surprisingly, the civilian women at Defense rated the overall position of women at Defense as virtually identical to the position of women at State. Moreover, the women at Defense gave their department higher ratings than they gave government as a whole. Looking toward the future, women at Defense were only marginally less optimistic than women at State.

However, in the uniformed services, sexual harassment remains one of the major problems. The military has had a long history of sexual harassment. For example, during World War II, women were subjected to dirty jokes, slander campaigns and obscene cartoons. Similarly, a 1990 report by the Defense Manpower Data Center indicated that close to two thirds of women on active duty had been subject to "uninitiated and unwanted sexual attention." Moreover, the report found women were reluctant to report the incidents because they feared reprisals or thought nothing would be done.

In 1992, disclosure of the Tailhook incident by Lt. Paula Coughlin focused public awareness on sexual harassment in the military. Lt. Coughlin had been the victim, along with approximately 90 other women, of a sexual attack by a group of male Navy aviators at their annual convention in September 1991. After being groped by the pilots while trying to walk down a hall, Lt. Coughlin reported the incident, but the investigating officers took virtually no action and the pilots stonewalled. Coughlin finally was forced to go public. The resulting investigation of the Navy's handling of the incident resulted in the resignations of the secretary of the navy and the chief of naval operations. Though 117 officers were implicated, virtually all charges were dismissed. Coughlin resigned her position in February 1994, claiming that the attack and the reaction to her going public had stripped her of her ability to serve. Several of those who testified at the hearing linked sexual harassment in the military to the exclusion of women from combat positions, arguing that until that policy is reversed women can never expect to be treated as equals. In fact, sexual harassment within the military seems to be increasing. A General Accounting Office (GAO) report released in March 1995 compared sexual harassment at the three service academies in 1993–94 with that in 1990–91 and found significant increases, particularly at the Naval and Air Force academies. Such harassment led to the resignation of Elizabeth Saum from the Air Force Academy after she was subjected to a mock rape staged as part of a sexual exploitation scenario that had been added to the survival training program in 1993. (This phase of the training was only discontinued this year.)

A male with responsibility in personnel matters whom the authors interviewed at Defense indicated that sexual harassment is not a problem limited to the military side of the department. Though the incidents he described were of a less serious nature, his attitude toward them suggests that complaints by civilian women may also be ignored or downplayed:

> *There is sexual abuse—but not the kind you could ever pin down. I think harassment is everywhere—I don't mean the real kind you would do anything about—I mean the innuendos, the comments all done in jest and those kinds of things [done] with the nicest motives but having the most terrible effect…. There is a generation who believes when a woman is attractive, they should pay her a compliment no matter what. So they, even during the course of a business meeting, might make a compliment not done maliciously, but it's done. It is a part of stereotypes those people have.*

The Clinton Administration has made efforts to improve the status of women. For example, in the Office of the Secretary of Defense, the special assistant to the secretary, the directors of defense research and engineering, reserve affairs and legislative affairs and three deputy under secretaries are all women. In addition, the Administration appointed the first woman as Air Force Secretary, Sheila Widnall. Women also hold two of the top positions in the Army and two in the Navy.

National Security Council

Since the NSC came of age during a time of somewhat more enlightened attitudes toward women, it has avoided the overt discriminatory policies against women of the State and Defense departments. However, because of the council's composition, there has been a virtual exclusion of women's participation. The first woman to break the barrier to the inner sanctum of this important center of foreign policy formulation was U.S. Ambassador to the UN Kirkpatrick, whom President Reagan invited to sit on the NSC. President Clinton has continued the practice of including the representative to the UN on the NSC, resulting in a second woman, Madeleine K. Albright, serving there.

While only two women have been members of the actual council, the staff, which is largely composed of political appointees, has been more open to women. In the Clinton Administration, several women have held important staff positions. Because other government agencies, notably State and Defense, are the other major source of advisers for the NSC staff, the prospects for more women serving depend heavily on the promotion and recognition of women in those departments.

Congress

Congress, too, has barriers to women's entry. However, most of the hurdles exist outside the institution and as a result few women are elected. For example, the Senate, the most important of the two houses in influencing foreign policy (due to its authority to ratify treaties and approve presidential appointments), has only had 23 women members, 6 of whom have been elected since 1992. The number of women elected to the House of Representatives is only somewhat better. Yet it was not until 1992 (the Year of the Woman) that women held 10 percent of House seats.

If one looks at the committees in the Senate and the House responsible for reviewing foreign policy issues, one sees the impact of internal rules on women's status. Party committees responsible for assigning new members to standing committees have tended to operate under traditional stereotypes about women's interests and abilities. Consequently, they have given few women positions on the "foreign policy" committees. Moreover, for the few women who have achieved such appointments, their limited time in Congress (nearly half of the women who have served in the Senate remained in office less than a year) has meant that none, to date, has acquired the seniority to move into the position of chair or ranking-minority member. Thus, the few women who have been, or are currently, serving on the foreign policy committees have generally not taken very influential or visible roles. The one possible exception is Representative Schroeder, who is currently the third-ranking Democrat on the National Security Committee. Schroeder has been a leading advocate for expanding opportunities for women in the military, including sponsoring legislation to remove combat restrictions on women.

The absence of women committee and subcommittee chairs has contributed to the limited movement of women into important staff positions. Not until 1995 was Congress under any obligation to avoid discrimination in hiring staff or to report on how many women it employs or in what positions they serve. An examination of recent staff members finds that only one woman, Marilyn A. Elrod, has ever been a top aide to a foreign policy committee. She was staff director for the House Armed Services Committee in the 103rd Congress.

3

Contemporary Women in Foreign Policy

THE NUMBER OF WOMEN entering federal employment and specifically the foreign policy realm is growing. Employment trends on the national and federal levels provide keys to what is happening within the foreign policy community. Nationally, the percentage of women employees had increased to 45 percent in 1992. The percentage of women in the federal workforce is only marginally lower. However, women in federal employment were overrepresented in clerical positions and underrepresented in administrative and professional categories (40 percent and 34 percent respectively in 1991). Moreover, women in the latter positions do not appear to be treated equitably, in that there is a significant wage gap between male and female employees that seems to be growing.

The percentage of women in federal employment declines the higher the rank of the position. This is particularly evident in the upper echelons of government employment, the Senior Executive Service (SES) and the Civil Service (General Schedule or GS) ranks leading up to the SES. (There are 18 grades in the Civil Service, with 01 being the lowest and 18 the highest.) The number of women at the SES rank remained restricted (less than 6 percent in 1978; 13 percent by 1993).

Table 1		
	1991	1993
Women in SES	12 percent	13.0 percent
Women in GS 15	13 percent	15.3 percent
Women in GS 14	17 percent	19.4 percent
Women in GS 13	22 percent	24.8 percent
Women in GS 12	29 percent	31.0 percent

Source for Tables 1 and 2: *Senior Executive Service*, Office of Personnel Management, Department of State, 1994.

To gauge the impact of women on foreign policy, it is necessary to examine more specifically where women are located within this process. Of course, having numerous women working in a particular agency, even high-ranking women, does not necessarily mean that those individuals are involved in foreign policymaking. However, the absence of women, especially at high levels, is a clear indication that women are not involved.

The number of women in the State and Defense departments has increased throughout the last two decades. Nevertheless women are still entering the field in fewer numbers than men. According to the government's annual reports, in 1983 women constituted 32 percent of all Defense Department employees and 37 percent of all State Department employees. Out of the total of 68 government agencies, in terms of their composite rankings for the employment of minorities and women, with 1 the highest, State ranked 39th, Army 45th, Navy 59th, Air Force 60th, and the Office of the Secretary of Defense (OSD) was at the bottom. Moreover, that year the State

Department's professional employees included only 19 percent women, and the professionals in the entire Defense Department were 13 percent female. As shown in Table 2, neither department has yet achieved a particularly high percentage of women in the SES.

Table 2: Percentages of Women in SES		
Department	1991	1993
State	16 percent	15 percent
Defense overall	6 percent	7 percent
OSD	9 percent	11 percent
Army	6 percent	6 percent
Air Force	6 percent	5 percent
Navy	4 percent	4 percent

Department of State

As of March 1993, the Department of State had 14,287 employees divided into two separate spheres, the Foreign Service and the Civil Service. The Civil Service, 39 percent of State Department personnel, manages the communications, logistics and stateside part of foreign relations, largely from Washington, D.C. The Foreign Service (61 percent) sends individuals to represent the United States around the world, in embassies, at international organizations and at various conferences and negotiations. Most of the professionals in substantive policymaking jobs in the State Department's Washington offices are in the Foreign Service. The Foreign Service itself is divided into "generalists" and "specialists." Generalists (35 percent of overall employees) are those usually referred to as diplomats or Foreign Service Officers. Specialists (26 percent) are those with specific skills, such as security personnel, budgetary officers or secretaries; they are not usually involved in foreign policy decisions.

Women tend to be heavily clustered in the Civil Service. For instance, in 1993, women made up 62 percent of the Civil Service but only 36 percent of Foreign Service specialists and 26 percent of Foreign Service generalists. In 1970, there were three women in the Senior Executive Service of the State Department; in 1981 there were eight; in 1987 there were nine; and in 1993 the number jumped to 17. However, taking into account the growth of the SES, there has been little or no progress in the percentage of women in the SES. Table 3 also shows a large percentage of women clustered at GS13, indicating that women encounter a glass ceiling that limits their entry into senior positions.

Table 3: Senior Level Civil Service—1993

	Total	Male	Female	% Female
SES	120	103	17	14.2
GS15	373	275	98	26.3
GS14	500	332	168	33.6
GS13	701	354	347	49.5

Source: Affirmative Action Accomplishment Report 1994.

It is the Foreign Service positions that are more relevant to foreign policy decisionmaking. According to the State Department's own reports, in 1957 there were 306 women Foreign Service Officers out of a total of 3,436, or 9 percent. After that the percentage of women officers actually declined, to 4.8 percent in 1970. By 1977 women rebounded with 337 women out of 3,514 officers, or 9.6 percent. By 1987, women finally got past a token status of 15 percent when they attained 23 percent. By 1990, women constituted 24 percent of the 4,954 FSOs.

The figures for recruitment are slightly more promising. In 1966, only 7 percent of the incoming Foreign Service candidates were women, but by 1987 the number of women recruits had reached 34 percent.

However, as Table 4 makes clear, the distribution of women has not been uniform at all ranks of employment. As in the Civil

Service, the senior ranks of the Foreign Service have consistently been male-dominated, with women constituting 12 percent of the SES and only 7 percent of the SFS in 1989. (FS ranks are the reverse of GS, where 01 is the bottom.)

Table 4: Women in the Foreign Service

	12/31/70		12/31/89	
	No. of women	% of women	No. of women	% of women
Senior FS	23	2.1	54	6.9
Middle FS 1–3	261	8.2	777	20.4
Junior FS 4–6	1,409	37.9	1,231	34.7

Source: "WAO'S 20th Anniversary: Legacy of the Past—Challenges for the Future" (Washington, D.C.: Women's Action Organization, 1990).

Within the Foreign Service, there are different distribution patterns for the generalists and specialists. Not only are there more women in the less influential specialist ranks, but both subdivisions (see Tables 5 and 6) show the continued pattern of women in the lower and middle ranks, and men in the senior grades. This is much more pronounced for the specialists.

Table 5: Foreign Service Personnel 1993/Generalists

Grade	Total Employees	No. of Women	Percentage Women
SFS	754	81	10.7
FS-01	821	162	19.7
FS-02-03	1977	584	29.5
FS-04-06	1517	496	32.7
FS-07-09	2	1	50.0
Total Generalists	5071	1324	26.1

Source: Affirmative Action Accomplishment Report 1994.

Table 6: Foreign Service Personnel 1993/Specialists

Grade	Total Employees	No. of Women	Percentage Women
SFS	68	2	2.9
FS-01	216	17	7.9
FS-02-03	1067	168	15.7
FS-04-06	1855	761	41.0
FS-07-09	465	402	86.5
Total Specialists	3739	1350	36.1
Total Generalists & Specialists	8810	2674	30.4

Source: Affirmative Action Accomplishment Report 1994.

As noted, within the Foreign Service it is the generalist corps that is most involved in substantive policy formulation. It is subdivided into four groups, or "cones"—political, economic, consular and administrative, of which the political and economic cones are considered the most prestigious and the most advantageous for promotion to the Senior Foreign Service. Until recently (when a tenuring system was adopted), officers were placed in a cone when hired. It was quite rare, but not impossible, to switch cones mid-career. Therefore, the assignment was of great importance. The State Department has been criticized for assigning women to less advantageous cones. In 1993 the percentage of women in each of the cones was as follows: administrative, 29 percent; consular, 35 percent; economic, 21 percent; and political, 19 percent. Looking at these assignments from another angle, of all women Foreign Service generalists in 1993, 24 percent were assigned to the political cone, 23 percent to the consular cone, and 18 percent were unconed. For all male Foreign Service Officers, the comparable figures were 35 percent, 15 percent and 12 percent.

That women FSOs had been disproportionately assigned to the consular cone has been recognized publicly in at least two places, in *Palmer et al.* v. *Christopher* and in the recently released GAO report on the Foreign Service requested by Congress. The latter stated that there is a "disproportionate number of minorities and white women in functional areas that employee groups consider to be less desirable." This overrepresentation of women in the consular cone could be a further obstacle to women's career advancement, since, as the GAO concluded, political and economic officers have the greatest chance of promotion.

Another specific group likely to have an impact on foreign policy is the ambassadors. The number of women in this group has remained small. In 1989, only 7 percent of the ambassadors were women. Under the Clinton Administration the figure was 9 percent as of September 1994. In the past, most women ambassadors served in smaller countries that were somewhat peripheral to U.S. interests. Clinton's women ambassadorial appointees hold posts at the UN, the Organization of American

States, Austria, France and the Czech Republic, among others. The hesitancy of Presidents to appoint women ambassadors stems from a number of variables. For career officers, the State Department's past policies that discriminated against women in terms of deputy-chief-of-mission appointments obviously hindered their further advancement. Secondarily, the assumption that an ambassador's wife will serve as embassy hostess has necessarily worked against women. The difficulty that women have in rising to the ambassadorial level is also compounded by the tendency of Presidents to utilize ambassadorships for political patronage. Recent Presidents, especially Bush and Clinton, have been heavily criticized for this practice.

The Defense Department

Despite the combat restrictions, the number of women in the active-duty forces has increased significantly since the 1970s. In 1971, according to Mady Segal, an expert on women in the military, women constituted only 1.6 percent of the total active-duty personnel. By 1993 women were 11.6 percent of the Department of Defense overall and 12.2 percent of the total number of officers, the persons most likely to be involved in decision-making. There is some slight expectation that the numbers of women will increase as the percentage of women recruits grew from 13 percent in 1991 to 15 percent in 1992 and 1993.

Women civilians employed within DOD have clustered in jobs in lower grades. Consequently, their inclusion in the policymaking ranks has been restricted. Most of the GS women are at GS-10 or below, a level from which few people are promoted into the managerial/policy grades. However, women made some, albeit limited, gains in entering the policymaking ranks, climbing from 2 percent of SES positions in 1979 to 6 percent in 1991 (see Table 7).

In the Defense Department the two central bureaucracies charged with formulating foreign policy are the Office of the Joint Staff (formerly known as the Office of the Joint Chiefs of Staff) and the Office of the Secretary of Defense. The former is dominated by military personnel; the service chiefs themselves

Table 7: Department of Defense Civilian Workforce—1991

Grade	Total Employees	Women (percentage of total)	
GS 1-4	78,360	60,286	(77%)
GS 5-8	200,577	141,478	(71%)
GS 9-12	291,816	97,296	(33%)
GS 13-15	25,800	4,289	(17%)
GS 16-18	7	0	(0%)
GS Total	596,560	303,349	(50%)
GM 13	33,036	6,228	(19%)
GM 14	18,966	2,398	(13%)
GM 15	9,359	790	(18%)
GM Total	61,361	9,416	(15%)
SES 1-2	130	19	(15%)
SES 3-4	1,079	54	(5%)
SES 5-6	273	15	(5%)
SES Total	1,482	88	(6%)
Total	659,403	312,853	(47%)

Source: Department of Defense, September 1991.
This table does not include all DOD employees. In particular, hourly wage and "blue collar" workers are not included, nor are consultants and other nonpermanent personnel. GM stands for General Manager.

have always been exclusively male. The personnel listings (*Federal Yellow Book*, 1995) show only six women in the Office of the Joint Staff, and they occupy positions as operations division chief, protocol officer, executive assistant, administrative officer and secretary. In terms of the entire Office of the Joint Staff civilian employees, fully 85 percent of the GS staff in 1991 were women, who typically dominate the administrative and secretarial staff, with men in management and analytical positions.

The same pattern prevails in the Office of the Secretary of Defense, which includes not only the immediate staff of the secretary and deputy secretary, but numerous policy and planning functions as well (see Table 8). Though women are 46 percent of total employees, they are clustered in the lower GS ranks, while SES is overwhelmingly male.

Table 8: Office of the Secretary of Defense Civilian Workforce—1991

Grade	Total Employees	Women (percentage of total)	
GS 1–4	2	1	(50%)
GS 5–8	331	319	(96%)
GS 9–12	149	126	(85%)
GS 13–15	9	7	(78%)
GS 16–18	0	0	
GS Total	491	453	(92%)
GM 13	137	25	(18%)
GM 14	104	50	(48%)
GM 15	528	101	(19%)
GM Total	669	176	(26%)
SES 1–2	21	5	(24%)
SES 3–4	171	15	(9%)
SES 5–6	83	9	(11%)
SES Total	275	29	(11%)
Total	1,435	658	(46%)

Source: Department of Defense, 1991.

"I know how you must feel, Ms. Willoughby, but sexual harassment is part of our cultural heritage."

National Security Council

The NSC brings together the most powerful and influential set of advisers for any President struggling with foreign policy issues. As noted previously, none of the official members of the NSC has been a woman, although Kirkpatrick and Albright have been included at the invitations of Presidents Reagan and Clinton respectively. The head of the NSC staff is assistant to the President for national security affairs, currently Anthony Lake. Below the national security adviser are two deputy assistants to the President, 20 special assistants and senior directors (in charge of Russian affairs, defense policy/arms control, etc.) and one executive secretary, who are all presidential appointees. Other employees include directors, executive specialists and administrative assistants. A number of women have served as prominent staff members in the past, including Condoleezza Rice, provost of Stanford University, and Madeleine Albright. As of January 1995, of the two deputy assistants, one is a woman, Nancy E. Soderberg, who is also staff director. Of the 20 special assistants, two are women (see Table 9).

Table 9: National Security Council Staff

	Total	Men	Women	%Women
NSC 1995				
Appointees	22	19	3	13.6
Other	60	35	25	41.7
Total	82	54	28	34.1
NSC 1990				
Appointees	15	14	1	6.7
Others	73	46	27	37.0
Total	88	60	28	31.8
NSC 1986				
Appointees	17	17	0	0
Other	53	33	20	37.7
Total	70	50	20	28.6

Source: *Federal Yellow Book*, 1986, 1990, 1995.

As the table demonstrates, there has been a very small number of women in the upper level of the NSC staff, though their percentage has increased from 0 in 1986 to 13.6 percent in 1995.

The Congress

One of the most striking things about women working in Congress is how few they are. Of these, less than a handful in the last three Congresses have served as members of the committees involved in national security policy. As Table 10 indicates, there has been a much higher percentage of women on committee staffs than among the members. This probably reflects the general increase in the numbers of women entering the field of foreign and defense policy (and the fact that it is much easier to be hired by a congressional committee than it is to run and win an election). However, these figures should be

Table 10: Committees of the U.S. Congress Representation of Women Members and Staff for 102nd/103rd/and 104th Congresses

Senate Committees	Total Members 102/103/104	Women Members 102/103/104	Total Staff[a] 102/103	Women Staff 102/103
Appropriations:				
Defense Subcommittee	18/17/17	0/0/0	10/9	2/1
Foreign Operations Subcommittee	13/13/13	1/2/2	4/4	1/1
Armed Services	20/22/21	0/1/1	37/30	6/5
Foreign Relations	20/20/18	1/1/3	8/22	1/7
Select Committee on Intelligence	17/17/17	0/0/1	5/3	1/0

House Committees	Total Members 102/103/104	Women Members 102/103/104	Total Staff[a] 102/103	Women Staff 102/103
Appropriations:				
Defense Subcommittee	13/13/13	0/0/1	13/13	2/4
Foreign Operations Subcommittee (National Security)[b]	12/12/14	0/2/0	3/5	2/0
Armed Services (National Security)[b]	55/56/55	4/4/4	59/54	23/17
Foreign Affairs (International Relations)[b]	45/45/43	2/5/3	31/37	9/14
Select Committee on Intelligence	21/19/16	1/1/1	16/12	4/3

Source: *Congressional Yellow Book*.

[a] Does not include those clearly identifiable as secretarial or administrative staff.
[b] Note many of the committees and subcommittees in the House underwent reorganization and name changes in the 104th Congress.

viewed with caution. Although those individuals clearly identified as secretaries were not included, many staff titles were so vague that it was difficult, if not impossible, to distinguish those with purely administrative duties from those with analytical and substantive responsibilities. Unlike the departments of State and Defense, the members of Congress have not been required to file EEO reports on the racial and gender composition of their staffs before 1995. Thus, this set of data must be regarded with a healthy caution.

4

Characteristics of Women in Foreign Policy

ALTHOUGH WOMEN have traditionally been excluded, some have made it into the elite foreign policy establishment and have had a significant impact. How did these women surmount the barriers that have prevented so many others from assuming positions of influence? And how did their career patterns differ from those of men? In order to answer these questions, the authors conducted interviews in 1988 with 79 persons in senior policymaking positions in the departments of State and Defense. (The tables below are based on that data.)

The Influence of Personal Factors

Most of the women in our sample were younger than men in similar positions (see Table 11). Over half the men were over 50 years of age, while only a third of the women were this old. Part of the explanation for the difference can be found in the cultural stereotypes mentioned in Chapter 1. Many older women, unlike older men, would not have pursued a career or chosen to work outside the home. Attitudes on the appropriateness of work for women were particularly reflected in the career histories of older women, many of whom reported that they did not so much plan a career as fall into one. Also contributing to the age discrepancy was the fact that until relatively recently policies adopted by State and Defense kept women out of both agencies.

Table 11: Age Distribution of All Women and Men (percent)

	60 or older	51–60	41–50	40 or under
Men	18.4	36.8	36.8	7.9
Women	7.5	25.0	42.2	25.0

The failure of some women to plan a career might also help explain the fact that the men in our sample were generally better educated than the women (see Table 12). These results parallel those found by the U.S. Merit Systems Protection Board in a large study of men and women employed by the federal government in 1992. One explanation for the education gap may be found in the difficulty women face in obtaining advanced degrees. Women have been less likely to receive fellowships for graduate study, making advanced education more difficult. Additionally, since many of the people in our sample reported that they worked on their advanced degrees while employed by the government, women would have been less likely to have had this opportunity, since their employment histories tended to be shorter and at lower levels. Furthermore, women with family responsibilities may find combining work with school harder to do than men. Regardless of the source of the gap, women may well be disadvantaged relative to men in their efforts to progress up the career ladder by their weaker educational background.

Table 12: Highest Degree of All Women and Men (percent)

	High School	Bachelors	Masters	Ph.D./MD/JD
Men	0.0	26.3	36.8	36.8
Women	2.4	29.3	48.8	19.5

In addition to not having an advanced degree, another educational handicap for women was the lack of scientific or mathematical training, perhaps due to stereotypes about women's abilities in these fields. Several of the men in technical offices who were interviewed reported that they had few women working in their area and did not expect that to change as long as women shied away from studying in these fields. This is particularly a problem for women at the Defense Department, where many of the positions require a technical degree at entry level. In Defense, only half as many women as men (20 percent and 39 percent respectively) had training in math, computers, science or a related field.

Table 13: Major of Highest Degree (percent)

Major	Women	Men
Political Science/ International Relations/Public Administration	52.5	39.5
Math/Accounting/Computers	10.0	7.9
Humanities	10.0	10.5
Law/Other Social Science	20.0	23.7
Science/Engineering/Medicine	2.5	13.1
Business	5.0	5.3

A higher proportion of women than men had degrees in government, political science or public administration. In the youngest group, 80 percent of the women, but none of the men, had their highest degree in this area. That many of the women pursued degrees in these traditionally male fields indicates that at a young age they showed interest in nontraditional careers and began to prepare for jobs in government. The burgeoning number of women obtaining degrees in these fields suggests there may be more women in government positions in the years to come.

Not surprisingly, virtually all the women and men in our sample had moved to their current jobs from another government position. Only a handful, mostly appointees, had come from private practice or industry, and a few got the job through family connections. Most of our respondents said their previous position involved foreign policy, although for the older group more men than women reported such experience. Men and women under 40 were equally likely to have had another foreign policy position. Younger women were thus more likely to have been educated for a position in government and foreign policy and to have had a consistent career path. As anticipated, restrictive cultural stereotypes and the practices of the State and Defense departments had their greatest impact on the older women.

Asked why they chose government work, respondents' answers varied widely (see Table 14). Women were considerably more likely to have mentioned political experience than men, although the difference could be partially attributable to the greater number of women appointees in our sample, several of whom had worked in Reagan's campaigns for governor of California and/or President and were subsequently rewarded with a position in Washington. Women were also more likely to have mentioned a previous governmental experience, either internships in government agencies while in college or graduate school, or positions in other agencies before coming to State or Defense. For men, often the key event in their lives that brought them into government was a stint in the military. This was particularly true for the men serving in intelligence in both the State and Defense departments, most of whom had served in that capacity during wartime.

Table 14: Factors Mentioned As Reasons/Motives for Choosing a Career in Government— All Men and Women (Departments of State and Defense)

	All Men %	All Women %
Political experience	2.6	14.6
Military experience	36.8	7.3
College experience	39.5	41.5
Industry experience	15.8	19.5
Government (including internship) experience	18.4	41.5
Educational experience	71.1	53.7
Service to country reason	36.8	24.4
Opportunity reason	18.4	34.1
Interest in government/politics/area reason	63.2	75.6
"Fell into it" reason	10.5	33.0
Family reason	18.4	31.7

In the related area of college experience, men and women showed fewer differences. As the following quote suggests, several men and a few women noted the key role played by professors or other academic mentors in helping them decide on a government career:

[It was a] series of accidents I suppose…. a professor of mine at [college] turned out to be what they call a spotter for the CIA and [he] put them in touch with me. [I] worked [several] years in the CIA as an analyst.

Shifting from experiences to reasons for joining government, there were no significant differences in the motives cited by the women and men. The first reason was service to country; men were somewhat more likely to cite this as a reason than women. The military background of the men may have been a factor in this regard. However, among the youngest group, it was the women who were more likely than the men to mention service, and none of the women in this age bracket had had a military background.

Turning to the other motives, there was a notable difference between men and women with regard to opportunity. Women career officials were much more likely than men in comparable positions to mention opportunities for advancement. For many of the interviewees, when they were starting their careers, the government was a more equitable employer than private industry. The following is a fairly typical scenario:

In 1962 I graduated from [college]. Equal pay for women was unheard of in industry. The government was the only employer offering equal salary for [equal] accomplishments.... But that was the primary reason I came to work for the government. I was very naive, and when I was in an interview with [a private company], I was shocked when the statement was made to me, 'For a woman we'll pay....' I'll never forget those words. They violated every sense of fairness I had. So I said a few four-letter words and stalked out of the interview. What did I know? I was just a poor little naive girl in [the South]. I'd never been out in the big world. The recruiter had no hesitation to put it into those words.

A woman who graduated in the 1950s recounted a related experience:

Frankly, when I got out of college in 1956, I was a political science major, the first thing I was asked on all of those interviews (where I was going to go out and save the world) was how fast can you type. Since I don't type very fast, I joined the Air Force,

> *because at least I found there I didn't have to type, and I got paid the same as the men got paid. In 1956 that was one of the few places that was true.*

What is clear in both of these quotes is that the women were influenced by the relative advantage of a career in the government or military over a job in industry. These women displayed a consciousness about discrimination long before the women's movement. Moreover, government recruiters seemed to be acting as if women were qualified for positions of some authority while private employers did not. A natural conclusion that might have been drawn was that women had more ability relative to government work than business.

Women, not surprisingly, were somewhat more likely to mention falling into a career rather than planning one. This was particularly true for the older women, 80 percent of whom reported they had no clear career plan. Among the younger group of women, those under 40, none of them said they "fell into their career." For the youngest women, the critical factor was often family-connected, such as encouragement by a parent or relative to follow a certain career. This was given by both men and women. Interestingly, none of the oldest group of women mentioned this kind of influence, perhaps because families of their generation were not supportive of daughters' careers, especially when they might involve travel abroad or the military. A second family reason, the need to accommodate one's career to that of a husband, was also found in the responses of women, especially young women. Several women recounted that they took their job in government so they could either be near their husband or put him through school:

> *My husband decided to come back to law school and get a Master's in taxation. So we came [to Washington] and I began applying for jobs. This was the first job I got, which was good because he wasn't working and neither was I.*

Especially since women at State who married before 1970

would have automatically lost their jobs in the Foreign Service, accommodating the dual-career couple is a modern-day phenomenon mentioned only by the younger respondents.

Actions by Individuals to Advance Careers

How did the women (and men) in the sample make it to the top of the foreign policy establishment? Respondents were queried about the tactics they used, specifically whether they had sought or been asked to take their current position. It was anticipated that the women in our sample would respond differently from the men for a number of reasons. First, women are generally thought to be less aggressive than men, though whether this is a product of socialization or genetic or hormonal factors is a matter of intense debate. Second, it has been argued that women are less likely than men to attribute their own success to their intelligence and abilities. Thus there is reason to expect that successful women might underestimate their own role in achieving their positions and therefore be less willing to take further action to move their careers forward.

The authors' study found that women, regardless of age or other category, were always less likely to report having actively sought their current position. Older women and women political appointees were particularly unlikely to have sought an advancement. This reluctance to seek out a promotion may also be the result of discouragement on the part of women who have already had to struggle to overcome so many barriers to their careers. More common, especially for the career women, was a pattern whereby they were aware of the position that was the next step and while they may not have asked for it, they did try to work hard so as to be recognized and therefore asked to take it.

Several of the respondents also volunteered comments about the relative availability and use of mentoring or networking as a tactic in securing their jobs. Many of the older women mentioned the lack of mentors, while the younger women often had male mentors. As one noted, she was forced to rely on men because she had no female colleagues who could serve in this

Table 15: Percentage of Respondents Who Sought or Were Asked to Take Current Position

	% Sought	% Asked	% Other (volunteered)
Overall			
Men	47.4	47.4	5.3
Women	26.8	56.1	17.1
Career Officials			
Men	51.6	41.9	6.5
Women	39.1	39.1	21.7
Political Appointees			
Men	28.6	71.4	0.0
Women	11.1	77.8	11.1
Age:			
Over 60			
Men	42.9	57.1	0.0
Women	0.0	66.7	33.3
50–59			
Men	42.9	50.	7.1
Women	20.0	80.0	0.0
40–49			
Men	50.0	42.9	7.1
Women	47.1	29.4	23.5
Under 40			
Men	66.7	33.3	0.0
Women	10.0	70.0	20.0

capacity. "One of my greatest regrets was the absence of a woman mentor. I think there simply weren't very many women when I was young. I've had lots of male mentors. I've never had a female mentor." Those who had good mentors could be very specific about the help they received. One woman at Defense who had several good mentors commented: "If you've got a good mentor...they can be worth their weight in gold, because they give you the proper perspective and balance."

Correspondingly, the absence of women mentors was often noted in trying to explain a person's lack of advancement:

It took me almost twice as long as my colleagues to attain the same level they attained. I had to work harder, to prove myself. Part of it is the 'old boy network.' They are very comfortable with the old people they know and to some of them women are unknown factors. We don't have an 'old girl network' at DOD [the Department of Defense].

Given the importance of mentors for women, it is not surprising that both the women who had been mentored, and those who had not been so lucky, often helped younger women. The dedication of the women who were interviewed to providing such support to younger women, hopefully, means the next generation of women in the foreign policy process may not have to struggle alone to make it to the top of their chosen profession.

Family Factors

The variables of marriage, pregnancy and children inevitably mean that women's career patterns will be significantly different from those of men. Studies have found that professional women tend more than men to be single, widowed, divorced or separated. The primary explanation for this phenomenon centers around the conclusion that, due to job discrimination and the competing requirements of household responsibilities, careers are ultimately more demanding for women, particularly careers which are highly taxing in terms of time and commitment. According to the role-conflict theory, one way of dealing with the strain experienced by those with ambitious careers plus competing home demands is to eliminate one of the roles. Thus those concentrating on a career may forgo marriage.

The same logic is also applied to having children: as the level of commitment and preparation required for a job rises, there is a general increase in the proportion of childless women and a corresponding decrease in the proportion of women with many children. The women managers at the State and Defense departments fit the expected pattern with regard to marriage and children fairly well (see Table 16).

Table 16: Marital and Parental Status of Women and Men in the Foreign Policy Arena

	Overall		Appointees		Careerists	
	Men	Women	Men	Women	Men	Women
Percent Currently Married	89.5	61.0	100.0	44.4	87.1	73.9
Percent with Children	89.5	53.7	100.0	38.9	87.1	65.2

The women in our sample seemed to be avoiding or delaying marriage. This was particularly true for the political appointees, of whom all the males were married, while less than half of the women were presently married. One appointee explained her decision not to marry as follows:

I spent years thinking that, of course, I want marriage and children, as everybody does, but always someplace off in the future, never right now. And then I spent years thinking that there must be something wrong with me because I didn't want marriage and children. And if the women's movement meant anything to me personally, it was realizing that there is nothing wrong with not wanting to have a family or to consider a career.

Women were also less likely to have children. The figures for children were also more skewed for appointees, with all the men, but barely a third of the women, having children. The percentage of career men and women with children were 87 percent and 65 percent respectively. That pattern has not changed. A very high percentage of women in the SFS today are single or married without children.

Not surprisingly, more than half the women (55 percent) who had families but only a quarter of the men (27 percent) found it difficult to combine a career with parenthood. Career women and men seemed to have greater problems than appointees, with two thirds of the women and almost a third of the men citing difficulties. Only 29 percent of the women appointees and a minuscule 14 percent of the men appointees indicated role conflict. One might speculate that appointees, because of their greater earning power or less structured career path, might have been able to manage more easily the two careers of professional and parent. One appointee indicated she had been able to have a family because she could afford live-in help. For those appointees and career women with young children at home, the range of problems associated with raising children and being in a high-powered career were familiar ones: lack of good child care, no free time, conflict between demands of the job and demands of parenting, travel and guilt. One woman described her experience as a young mother as follows:

> *I was one of a very few working mothers; many said it was a mistake. I was able to accomplish what I did by trying to be a superwoman. I worked 22 hours a day. The workload was backbreaking. I went through [my] twenties and thirties feeling exhausted. I went to the doctor for vitamin and iron shots because I never had any energy. I stayed in a job nine years, which was not the best career move, but it didn't require overtime or travel.*

A single mother's response is even more poignant in describing the trade-offs she had to make:

> *[I] hired women housekeepers because I was a single parent since he was four years old. I was like most male executives, I had no idea what was happening to my kid. Someone else was taking care of him. It wasn't until the last couple of years, before I*

started to pay attention to him. My career had gotten down to earth, I'd gone as far as I was going. I had an awful lot of male friends whose kids had disappeared and they were sorry they had never seen them.

Interestingly, several of the younger men reported some problems combining roles too. One man at Defense responded:

I don't feel I have enough time with children. Most stressful aspect of my life is the competition between my career and my kids, and resolving that conflict. [I'm] always compromising—painful no matter which one gets the short end of the stick.

An older man, however, was frankly surprised by the question regarding problems combining career and parenthood. He replied, "No. But I don't know how to answer that question as a man. That's sort of a strange question to ask. I'm supposed to do that [pursue career]." One might expect this attitude to influence this man's view of women colleagues who do work and have children. Indeed, several of the women in other parts of the interview noted that they encountered colleagues and bosses who indicated that the women either could not manage a career and parenting or should not attempt to combine both.

Differences That Count

The impact of individual factors can also be measured in terms of career success. In particular, women were not as likely as men to achieve their career goals, and women reported more partial than complete successes. This was particularly true for career women in both State and Defense, but especially in Defense where only 23 percent of them achieved their goals completely. This compared with 64 percent of the men indicating complete success and 91 percent partial or complete goal attainment. Among political appointees, all the women and men reported total or partial success. Thus, there is some indication that the barriers noted above do limit women's ability to achieve all they hoped to accomplish. A quote from a woman at

Defense conveys some of the difficulties encountered by women: "But your job is much more difficult. You have to beat them at their own game. They go around you, and it is a game. It takes longer for you to defeat them at the game and to get anything done. But unfortunately that is the way it works." The 1992 glass-ceiling study by the U.S. Merit Systems Protection Board that examined the barriers to women's advancement in the federal government substantiates these results. Even adjusting for women's lower levels of education, less time on the job and fewer relocations, women were still less likely to be promoted than men. A key factor to explain this seems to be the presence of children. Women with family responsibilities and women in the early stages of their careers, who might soon take on family responsibilities, experienced significantly fewer promotions. Managers seemed to be concluding these women could not (or would not) work the overtime hours required to move up to the top of the management ranks. These lower promotion rates of young women and women with children also help to explain the lack of older women and women with children in the higher levels of State and Defense.

The barriers women face have thus tended to impact on the extent to which women can shape foreign policy. In response to a specific question as to whether being a woman had limited their ability to have influence, over one third felt it did (although the vast majority of women did not feel so limited). There were significant departmental differences: in the State Department one in five answered in the affirmative, while among women in the Defense Department, the figure was closer to one in two. Most of the women respondents felt that women have to work harder than men and must continuously strive to prove themselves.

While some of these differences are disconcerting, it should be remembered that many of the disparities in the background of the men and women at the State and Defense departments were sharper for the older generations. The greater similarities between the sexes in the younger groups would lead one to expect fewer differences among women and men already in the career funnel at both departments, although the possibility exists that managers, acting as if women and men employees are differently committed to their work, might continue to restrict the upward mobility of women.

5

Conclusions and Prospects

A NUMBER OF FACTORS militate against a quick reversal of the historical pattern that shows women severely underrepresented at the highest level of the American foreign policy establishment. There are still all too few women among the ranks of the leaders and decisionmakers primarily due to cultural attitudes, both within the major foreign policy establishment and in the larger public. Even with more women entering Defense, State, the NSC and Congress, the tendency has been to restrict women to policymaking positions in more traditional support roles or to issues more tied to their supposed nurturing abilities. Thus, in Defense there are women in legal and personnel positions, in State women are disproportionately located in the consular and administrative cones, and in Congress women are assigned to committees that focus on domestic concerns, notably health and welfare issues. Therefore, even when an increasing number of women enter

"IF I MUST BE LONELY, I'D RATHER BE LONELY AT THE TOP!"

Rothco Original

these institutions, they are most often on the periphery of the foreign policy process.

More ominous is the near absence of women in the upper levels of decisionmaking. This is most apparent in the failure to ever have a woman serve as President, secretary of state, secretary of defense or national security adviser. Nor have there ever been any women chairs of major foreign policy committees in the House or Senate. The layer below these positions has also witnessed a near virtual exclusion of women. While the cultural stereotypes are important reasons for the absence of women at the top, structural barriers also have made, and possibly will for some time make, it difficult for women to break into the visible positions within the foreign policy establishment.

Within Congress, the structural barriers have been twofold: the failure of women to be elected and the rule of seniority restricting the selection of chairpersons to members with many years of service. Because men dominate among incumbents, women have had a difficult time breaking into the institution. Recent elections have seen incumbent advantages diminish, opening up more seats to women, but without the adoption of term limits, significant increases in the numbers of women in Congress cannot be expected. Moreover, because women are relatively recent arrivals to the institution, they have not been able to build up seniority, and seniority has been the ticket to committee chairs. This, too, is weakening with the adoption of term limits for chairs in the House, but the virtual exclusion of women from the relevant committees means that many women will not soon become leaders of major foreign policy committees.

Presidents' Appointees

Within the executive branch, the key to women's upward mobility is the President and his commitment to gender equity. To date, the President with the best record in his first year in office is Clinton. Thirty-one percent of Clinton's first year appointments went to women. Bush followed in second place with 20 percent, while under Reagan and Carter women constituted 12 and 14 percent, respectively, of their initial-year appointments. Although Clinton's overall record is good, like his predecessors he has appointed considerably fewer women to the Defense and State departments than his overall record would suggest. Out of appointments requiring Senate approval to 15 Cabinet-level departments, State was tied for 12th with 22 percent women and Defense ranked 13th with 19 percent women. Among the top foreign policy advisers, Clinton appointed only one woman, Albright. Yet relying on presidential appointments to promote women can be a double-edged sword. When appointments go to political allies instead of career officials, it merely contributes to the glass ceiling that women careerists face and to the lack of opportunities for government officials.

The President can also shape the role of women in the way he structures the foreign policy team and conducts foreign policy. To the extent the President places reliance on the traditional bureaucratic structures of State and Defense, the upward mobility of women in these departments will result in their greater influence. However, if the President restricts the foreign policy decisionmakers to an inner circle of close (and high-ranking male) advisers (as did President Bush), then women may find themselves still without a voice.

For most of U.S. history, women have been excluded from the institutions responsible for shaping and implementing foreign policy. Their relatively recent entry into these institutions has not yet resulted in equality. But times may be changing. As Genta Hawkins Holmes, director-general of the Foreign Service, recently stated:

Women have made great progress in the Department of State during the past two decades. In part that is due to cultural changes in our society that make it more acceptable for women to work in previously exclusive male preserves like diplomacy; the stunning success of women such as Rozanne Ridgway [former career diplomat, assistant secretary of state and president of the Atlantic Council]; and, also, the push from the courts. Women will continue to make progress because the cultural change has moved from mere acceptance of women to the necessity of women in the workplace and because the culture of the department is also changing toward acceptance of women as equal colleagues.

While many of the trends suggest that women are poised to rectify their historical exclusion, there persist many cultural and structural barriers to full equality. Consequently, women must keep pressing for inclusion. They cannot wait for men to open the door and invite them into the foreign policy process. In fact, many recent events suggest that there currently is a growing backlash against the gains women have made, particularly in areas traditionally seen as male preserves. Several strategies for change thus need to be pursued.

First, women must educate themselves for positions of influence. The data suggests that this is just what many young women are doing. Currently, two out of five undergraduates receiving degrees in political science and six out of ten undergraduates in international relations are women. At the graduate level, 40 percent of the master's degrees and 25 percent of the Ph.D.'s in both fields are being earned by women. Many women therefore have the academic preparation to enter the governmental institutions charged with formulating foreign policy. Similarly, women are also beginning to earn the degrees in mathematics and sciences that will be especially helpful for careers at the Defense Department. Though women are still getting few degrees in engineering, in mathematics nearly one half of the undergraduates are women and in the physical sciences, one third. However, in both fields only one in five Ph.D.'s are being earned by women. Second, women must actively pursue careers in government by volunteering to run for public office, applying for positions in the executive branch, and supporting those who do. Organizations such as Emily's List, a bipartisan organization in Washington, D.C., that promotes and raises funds for women political candidates, have been created for such an express purpose. Moreover, once in these positions, women must seek appointments to the relevant committees in Congress and promotions in the executive branch.

Third, women in positions of influence must continue to push for the inclusion of women in the foreign policy process and for an end to discrimination against women by these institutions. Representative Schroeder and Alison Palmer have done this in the past. More recently, Albright has spoken out about the need for the "equal and full participation by women in formulating policy and making political decisions." Targeting her own institution, the UN, for its failure to fully and equally recruit and utilize women, Albright concluded in a speech before the Commission on the Status of Women:

> *We look forward to working with the delegations from all nations, with the Secretariat and with outside organizations to energize this institution, and to bring about the full participation of women in policy formulation and decisionmaking. This is but*

one step toward the larger goal of sustaining progress toward equal rights and protections for women around the globe.

Fourth, women must organize both inside and outside the institutions of policymaking to push continually for the advancement of women in the field of foreign policy. Several organizations are currently very actively doing this. Women in International Security at the University of Maryland in College Park, the Women's Foreign Policy Council in New York City, the Women's Foreign Policy Group in Washington, D.C., the Women's Action Organization in the State Department and the Defense Advisory Committee on Women in the Services, as well as many individuals, serve to promote women in foreign policy and to encourage cooperation and networking.

Lastly, society must develop structures that allow women and men to manage both a high-powered career and a family life. Laws like the Family and Medical Leave Act, which requires businesses to give workers up to 12 weeks of unpaid leave for family and medical emergencies, are but one small example of the changes that need to be made. Because the burdens of family still fall disproportionately on women, they discourage women's role in foreign policy. Absent these reforms, women, and increasingly men, will have to choose between taking an active role in the nation's foreign affairs and raising a family.

Talking It Over
A Note for Students and Discussion Groups

This issue of the HEADLINE SERIES, like its predecessors, is published for every serious reader, specialized or not, who takes an interest in the subject. Many of our readers will be in classrooms, seminars or community discussion groups. Particularly with them in mind, we present below some discussion questions—suggested as a starting point only—and references for further reading.

Discussion Questions

There are several cultural values that have historically kept women out of the foreign policy process. What are these values? Do you think they have diminished sufficiently to no longer serve as barriers?

Women have faced some difficulties even getting admitted to institutions responsible for formulating foreign policy. What practices or rules have kept women out of the departments of

State and Defense, the National Security Council and the relevant congressional committees?

What current policies of these institutions make it difficult for women to move up through the ranks of the foreign policy establishment?

What personal sacrifices have women had to make to succeed in the departments of State and Defense? Are women and their opinions treated equally when they achieve the leadership positions in both departments?

Annotated Reading List

Calkin, Homer, *Women in the Department of State: Their Role in American Foreign Affairs*. Washington, D.C., Department of State, 1987. An overview of the status of women in the State Department through the mid-1970s.

Congressional Yellow Book. Washington, D.C., Monitor Publishing, Winter 1995. Along with its companion, the *Federal Yellow Book* (Washington, D.C., Monitor Publishing, Winter 1995), is a good source of statistics on women in the government.

Elshtain, Jean Bethke, *Women and War*. New York, Basic Books, 1987. An interesting discussion of the historical and philosophical foundations in Western culture that link men to war and women to peace.

Ewell, Judith, "Barely in the Inner Circle: Jeane Kirkpatrick." *Women and American Foreign Policy: Lobbyists, Critics, and Insiders*. New York, Greenwood Press, 1987. A brief profile of an important figure in the history of women in foreign policy.

Holm, Jeanne, Maj. Gen. USAF (Ret.), *Women in the Military: An Unfinished Revolution*. Novato, Calif., Presidio, 1982. A fascinating discussion of the history of women in the military by a woman who has lived through many of the changes.

Holsti, Ole R., and Rosenau, James N., "The Foreign Policy Beliefs of Women in Leadership Positions," *The Journal of Politics*, May 1981. The first of several articles that explore the differences between the foreign policy beliefs of men and women.

Kegley, Charles W., and Wittkopf, Eugene R., *American Foreign Policy: Pattern and Process*, 4th ed. New York, St. Martin's Press, 1991. One of many good books detailing how foreign policy is made in the United States.

McGlen, Nancy E., and Sarkees, Meredith Reid, *Women in Foreign Policy: The Insiders*. New York, Routledge, 1993. Relying on interviews with men and women at the State and Defense departments, examines the problems faced by women and the different beliefs and management styles of the two sexes.

Olmsted, Mary S., Baer, Bernice, Joyce, Jean, and Prince, Georgianna M., *Women at State: An Inquiry into the Status of Women in the United States Department of State*. Washington, D.C., Women's Research and Education Institute of the Congressional Caucus for Women's Issues, 1984. A good account of the early fight to improve the status of women at State.

Tickner, J. Ann, *Gender in International Relations: Feminist Perspectives on Achieving Global Security*. New York, Columbia University Press, 1993. The first of many books written by women scholars exploring the possible impact the perspective of women might have on the study of foreign policy.

U.S. Merit Systems Protection Board, *A Question of Equity: Women and the Glass Ceiling in the Federal Government*. Washington, D.C., U.S. Merit Systems Protection Board, October 1992. An examination of the problems women face in securing promotions in the federal government.